Forewo

by Squadron Leader David Thomas

Photo: Pam Thomas

I am delighted to be asked to write a foreword for this superb album of photographs taken by members of the Club and offered to you all as yet another revenue raising activity to keep XH558 flying. The £1.3million raised for 'Roll Out' in 2006 and yet another £1 million pledged recently by fans of the Vulcan is simply outstanding. This is yet one more example of the magnificent support the members of Vulcan to the Sky Club have given the 'Return to Flight' project over the years. I know that without the Club and its membership the struggle to return XH558 to the air would have been much harder and would probably have failed.

In all my privileged years flying in the display circuit I have never met a more loyal and generous fan base than Vulcan supporters. I hope you enjoy these photos graciously supplied by the avid Vulcan to the Sky Club membership base. 2008 was a very special year for me and my last as a Vulcan Display Pilot. It was a year that I shall always remember with great fondness and am sure with the help of this album will live on in the memories of thousands of aviation fans for years to come.

David Thomas

Photo left and front cover: Tom 'TJ' Hill

3

From the Club Chairman

It is a great pleasure to be able to write a few words about this superb album, which I am sure will be a 'must have' souvenir; bringing to life the story of the much awaited and vaunted return of XH558 to her rightful place - in the sky - displaying during the Summer of 2008.

Mirroring the comments made by Squadron Leader David Thomas in his Foreword, I must thank our loyal and dedicated Vulcan To The Sky Club members, both for their contributions to this book and for their unstinting support over the years, because, without doubt, they have played a significant part in the return of XH558 to the public domain.

My very best wishes to you all: it is a great privilege to be part of such a magnificent organisation and to serve as Chairman.

Richard Clarke
Chairman
Vulcan to the Sky Club

Photo: Tom 'TJ' Hill

Vulcan to The Sky Club

The 'Vulcan 558 Club' was launched in May 1997 in response to the public's continuing interest in the conservation of XH558 - the last Avro Vulcan to be retired by the RAF - at its home at Bruntingthorpe Aerodrome, Leicestershire.

From the outset, the Club sought to promote awareness of the preservation status of XH558 during its years as a ground-running and exhibition aircraft within the British Aviation Heritage collection. 1999 saw the Club actively endorse the XH558 Return to Flight project and, in 2000, the Club was formally registered as a Vulcan Operating Company (VOC) Founding Sponsor. The Club's support has delivered significant funds to the VOC and its successor, the Vulcan To The Sky Trust (VTTST). Renamed as the 'Vulcan To The Sky Club', it has been and continues to be a constant presence at airshows and other public events, thereby maintaining the high profile of XH558.

The Vulcan To The Sky Club forms the primary channel for public support of the VTTST and is a key funding source for XH558's flying activities and related education programme, helping the Trust deliver on its goals of both inspiring and educating in the fields of Cold War history and British engineering excellence.

The membership of the Club now stands at nearly 8,000 people and continues to grow daily, as both aviation enthusiasts and the general public alike join to express the importance of keeping XH558 flying.

Becoming a member of the UK's fastest growing aviation club could not be easier; some of the benefits and prices are shown below:

Join us today!

Membership Benefits

▲ Bi-annual full colour magazine 'The Vulcan' with exclusive articles, interviews and photographs

▲ Quarterly newsletters with the latest updates on flight plans and both Club and Trust activities

▲ Privileged access to XH558 and her crew

▲ Membership social events, both local and national

▲ Exclusive Club members visits to aviation-related places of interest

▲ Opportunities to work as 'Valued Volunteers' and 'Education Ambassadors'

▲ Access to Club Area on the VTTST website, including the forums

Membership Categories

▲ Adult - £24 per annum

▲ Family (max 2 adults & 2 children) - £24 per annum

▲ Senior (over 60) - £21 per annum

▲ Overseas - £29 per annum

1st year fees include £3 for membership pack.

How to join us

▲ At the Club stand at airshows and events

▲ Online at www.vulcantothesky.org

▲ Call 0116 247 8145

▲ Write to: Vulcan To The Sky P.O. Box 7263, Leicester LE5 6YR

The Return

It is 12:27pm on 18th October 2007. Around 250 people at Bruntingthorpe Airfield are holding their breath, anticipating an event unsurpassed in heritage aviation. A motionless Vulcan bomber sits on the runway, its crew completing their final checks. The four Rolls Royce Bristol Olympus turbojets spool up to 80%, then, as she begins moving, the throttles open further and the unmistakeable howl of the 200 Series Olympus rends the air. In front of the small crowd Avro Vulcan XH558 surges into the sky, desperate to be free of the ground that has shackled her for over fourteen years. The gathered guests simultaneously burst into applause, tears and superlatives, reactions reflected by those congregating in the lanes and fields around the airfield, whilst cameras record the moment: the world has a flying Vulcan once more!

XH558 became the first Vulcan B.Mk2 to join the RAF in 1960, and the last to leave in 1993. In service she was a training aircraft with No. 230 Operational Conversion Unit, a nuclear bomber, a maritime spook and an air-to-air tanker, before joining the Vulcan Display Flight and performing at airshows from 1986 onwards. Over 200,000 public signatures were submitted to the government in 1992, petitioning the Ministry of Defence to retain XH558, but to no avail. With an expensive Major Service looming, the decision to retire the Vulcan was taken. On 23rd March 1993, following a three and a half hour sortie around the type's old haunts, XH558 was delivered to her new owners, C. Walton Ltd. at Bruntingthorpe, Leicestershire. The 700C logbook was signed off and for the first time in 37 years the RAF no longer held an Avro Vulcan on their charge.

For the majority of aircraft this would have been the end, but the Vulcan is special: it is the People's Aircraft, revered with a love equal to that bestowed upon the Swordfish, Spitfire, Lancaster and Concorde. A volunteer maintenance group was formed, followed by a fledgling club, then a Trust and eventually the closed doors at the CAA and BAe Systems began to open. Finally, an agreement in principle was reached that XH558 could be returned to flight. Large sums of public money supplemented Heritage Lottery funding, philanthropic donations and aviation industry support, and after the most intensive, complex aircraft restoration ever undertaken, that monumental day in October 2007 arrived.

One year on, XH558 has completed her test flights, has been awarded her Permit to Fly and is active on the civil register as G-VLCN. She has been seen by more than one and a half million people at airshows the length of Britain, from the Channel Islands to Leuchars, with the "Vulcan Effect" swelling audiences by an estimated 20%. This book is a photographic record of XH558's return to our skies, a celebration of a momentous year in aviation, and a fitting tribute to the team who achieved what many considered impossible and returned a true British icon to the public. Long may she continue to fly.

Paul Gulliver, October 2008.

First Flight

18th October 2007

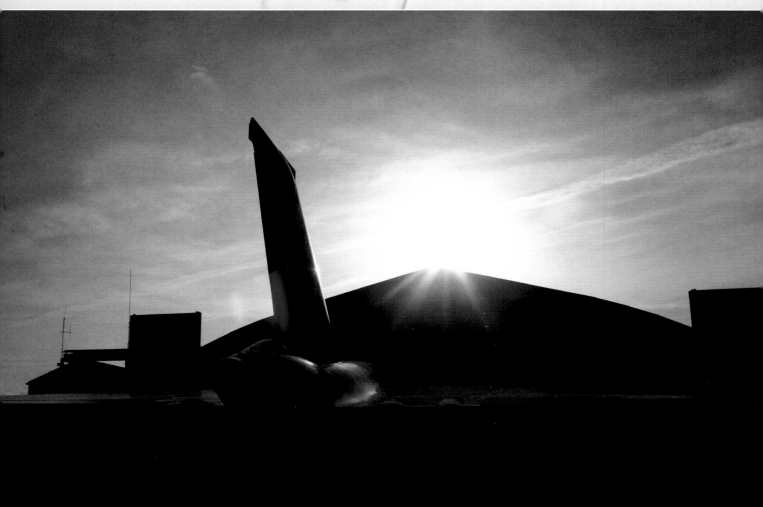

Airtesting begins

Photos, page 10: main picture Jim Camwell, insets John Richardson (1-2) and Jim Camwell, page 11: Tom 'TJ' Hill

*Photos, page 12
Tony Gardner,
page 13: main picture
Tom 'TJ' Hill, insets
Tom 'TJ' Hill and
Mark Freshney*

Photos, pages 14-15: main picture MoD/Crown Copyright, insets: Tom 'TJ' Hill and Richard Clarke/MoD/Crown Copyright

Photos: Tom 'TJ' Hill

*Photos, page 18: Ian Mulford,
page 19: top Tom 'TJ' Hill,
bottom John Richardson*

*Photos, page 20: from top
Tom 'TJ' Hill, Ian Mulford
and Tony Gardner,
page 21: from top Ian Mulford,
Tom 'TJ' Hill and Tony Gardner*

2008 Public Displays

*Photos, page 22: Tom 'TJ' Hill,
page 23: main image
Ava Richardson,
insets Steffie Hilgers*

RAF Waddington Airshow
First Public Display 5-6th July 2008

Photos: Tom 'TJ' Hill

*Photos, page 26: from top, Gill Silburn,
Tony Gardner and Tom 'TJ' Hill,
page 27: Tom 'TJ' Hill*

28

*Photos, page 28: Tom 'TJ' Hill,
page 29: main image Tony Gardner,
insets Tom 'TJ' Hill and Richard Clarke*

Photos, page 32: Tom 'TJ' Hill,
page 33: from top Mark Freshney,
Tom 'TJ' Hill and Gill Silburn

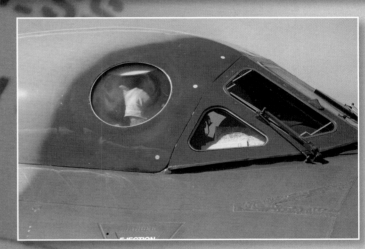

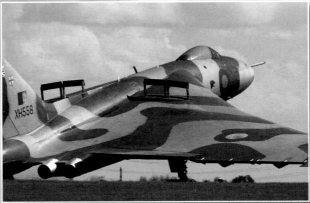

Photos, page 34: Mark Freshney,
page 35: main image Ava Richardson,
insets Tony Gardner

Photos: Tom 'TJ' Hill

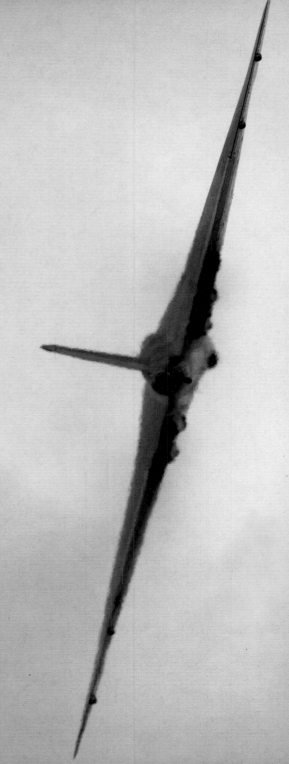

Farnborough
International Airshow

60th Anniversary
14-20th July 2008

Photos, page 38: main image
Tom 'TJ' Hill, insets from top
Richard Clarke and Tom 'TJ' Hill

Photos, page 39:
main image Tom 'TJ' Hill,
inset Lee Broadbent

Photos, page 42: main image Tom 'TJ' Hill, insets from left Tom 'TJ' Hill and Mark Freshney

Photos, page 43: main image Paul Gulliver,
insets from left Richard Clarke and John Richardson

Photos: Tom 'TJ' Hill

44

Marham, Cottesmore & Lowestoft
24th & 25th July 2008

Photos, pages 46-47:
Damien Burke, insets Tom 'TJ' Hill

*Photos, page 48:
top Tom 'TJ' Hill, bottom
Gary Stedman*

Photos, page 49:
top and bottom
Gary Stedman,
inset Tom 'TJ' Hill

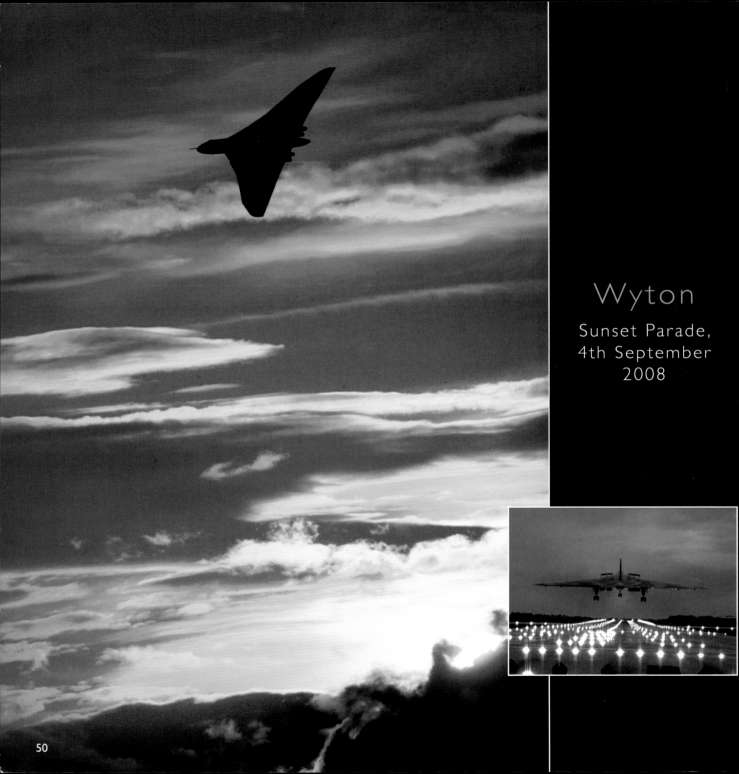

Wyton

Sunset Parade,
4th September
2008

Photos, page 50:
Damien Burke,
inset Paul Cooper,
page 51:
Damien Burke

Leuchars Airshow
13th September 2008

Photos: Andrew Blockley

Sywell

In formation with the Blades aerobatic team,
18th September 2008

Farnborough

Cody Centenary, 16th October 2008

On 16th October 1908, Samuel F. Cody became the first
man to carry out a controlled sustained flight in a powered
aircraft in Great Britain, piloting his Army Aeroplane No. 1
at Farnborough.

Enjoying the Summer...

with the Royal Air Force

For the duration of the 2008 airshow season, XH558 enjoyed the hospitality of the RAF at the forward operating bases of Waddington and Brize Norton.

The aircraft's stay at Waddington was particularly appropriate, given that she was originally delivered to RAF Waddington in 1960 and ended her service life there with the Vulcan Display Flight in 1993.

*Photos, page 56: Ian Waudby,
page 57: top/bottom Ian Waudby,
middle Tom 'TJ' Hill*

XH558

Photos, page 58: Tom 'TJ' Hill,
page 59: from top Mike Crompton
and Ian Waudby

Photos, page 60: John Richardson,
page 61: Ian Waudby, inset Paul Gulliver

Photos, page 62: Paul Gulliver,
page 63: main image Jim Camwell,
insets David Abbott and Ian Waudby

Photo: Bob Franklin

The last flight of 2008

On 12th November 2008, XH558 soared into the skies above Farnborough, embarking upon a circuitous route home to Bruntingthorpe, including "thank you" flypasts at a number of venues. Despite the success of the 2008 season and the "Vulcan Effect" markedly swelling airshow audiences, ongoing funding difficulties left many concerned that XH558's return to Bruntingthorpe may prove to be her final flight.

Photo: Gary Parsons

The Vulcan to the Sky Trust, supported by the Vulcan to the Sky Club, turned to the public to help them bridge the £1 million 2009 operational budget shortfall by March, via a pledge campaign.

In the face of tough economic conditions, Club volunteers worked tirelessly to promote awareness of XH558's plight and secure the required pledges. A fantastic conclusion to the campaign featured significant media support and coverage and saw the £1 million target achieved, with an incredible £500k pouring in over the final week!

Following the success of the pledge campaign, full-scale planning for the 2009 airshow season resumed, with XH558's pre-display servicing beginning on 20th April. The young and the old alike will be delighted and enthralled once more by the sight, sound, grace, beauty and power of Avro Vulcan XH558 in her rightful place in the sky!

XH558 flights in 2008

April 14th	Test flight, Bruntingthorpe to Cottesmore
April 16th	Test flight, Cottesmore to Bruntingthorpe
May 6th	Test flight, Bruntingthorpe to Coningsby
May 9th	Test flight, Coningsby to Bruntingthorpe
June 9th	Test flight, Bruntingthorpe
June 23rd	Test flight, Bruntingthorpe
July 3rd	Bruntingthorpe to Waddington (Permit to Fly and Display Authority obtained)
July 5th	Waddington (XH558's first airshow display since 1992)
July 10th	Waddington to Farnborough (display practice) and return
July 12th	Waddington to Farnborough
July 16th	Farnborough (display)
July 18th	Farnborough (display)
July 19th	Farnborough (display)
July 20th	Farnborough (display)
July 21st	Farnborough to Waddington
July 24th	Waddington to Marham (display), Lowestoft (display) and return
July 25th	Waddington to Cottesmore (display), Lowestoft (display) and return
August 22nd	Waddington to Brize Norton via Lancaster (flypast in memory of Lynne Braithwaite)
September 4th	Brize Norton to Wyton (Sunset Parade display) and return
September 6th	Brize Norton to Duxford (display) and return (display at Brize Norton Party in the Park)
September 7th	Brize Norton to Southport (display) and return
September 11th	Brize Norton to Jersey (display) and return
September 12th	Brize Norton to Leuchars (practice display)
September 14th	Leuchars to Brize Norton
September 18th	Brize Norton to Sywell (formation flights with the Blades aerobatic team), Lyneham (flypast) and return
October 16th	Brize Norton to Farnborough (Cody Centenary Event flypast)
November 12th	Farnborough to Bruntingthorpe